Cultural Traditions in

Sweden

Natalie Hyde

Crabtree Publishing Company
www.crabtreebooks.com

Crabtree Publishing Company

www.crabtreebooks.com

Author: Natalie Hyde
Publishing plan research and development:
  Reagan Miller
Editor: Rebecca Sjonger, Kelly Spence
Proofreader and indexer: Wendy Scavuzzo
Photo research: Tammy McGarr
Production coordinator and prepress technician:
  Tammy McGarr
Print coordinator: Margaret Amy Salter

Cover: A couple in traditional costume at midsummer (left); Swedish flag (top left); Maypole (left background); Christmas Celebration (centre); Boiled crayfish (bottom left); Cooked goose (bottom left); Herring (bottom middle); Christmas safron buns (bottom right) A girl dressed as an Easter Witch (right); Decorated Easter branches (right background)

Title page: Girls celebrating the National day of Sweden in Norrkoping. (Background) Buildings in the famous square Stor Torget in Stockholm, Sweden.

Photographs:
Alamy: ©Prisma Bildagentur: p 16
Getty Images: ©Miriam Glans: p 31
iStock: p21
Shutterstock: ©Anna-Mari West: front cover (middle right); ©Vlada Z: p12; ©Conny Sjostrom: front cover (middle left, middle bottom); p20, p21 (top); ©Piotr Wawrzyniuk: p26; ©Conny Sjostrom: p26, p28 (bottom); front cover (top left, middle left, botton right, bottom left, bottom middle), title page (background), pp4, 5, 6 (inset & bottom), 8 (bottom), 9 (inset), 11, 12, 14, 15 (bottom), 17, 23, 25, 27, 28, 30
Superstock: p13 (right); p15 (top right): Steve Skjold: p27 (top); p29 (left); Nordic Photos: p30 (left)
Thinkstock: ©Rolf_52: title page (girls); ©LoooZaaa: pp6 (top); 7, 8 (inset), 9 (top), 15 (top left), 25, 29 (right)
Wikimedia Commons: Christian Albrecht von Benzon: p10; Reindeer race, Tromso / Norway: p13 (top left); Bengt Nyman: pp18 & 19; p22 (left); Lapplaender: p22 (inset)

Library and Archives Canada Cataloguing in Publication

Hyde, Natalie, 1963-, author
    Cultural traditions in Sweden / Natalie Hyde.

(Cultural traditions in my world)
Includes index.
Issued in print and electronic formats.
ISBN 978-0-7787-8064-9 (bound).--ISBN 978-0-7787-8069-4 (pbk.).--
ISBN 978-1-4271-9962-1 (pdf).--ISBN 978-1-4271-9957-7 (html)

    1. Holidays--Sweden--Juvenile literature. 2. Festivals--Sweden--Juvenile literature. 3. Sweden--Social life and customs--Juvenile literature. I. Title. II. Series: Cultural traditions in my world

GT4861.A2H93 2015   j394.269485   C2014-907794-7
                                            C2014-907795-5

Library of Congress Cataloging-in-Publication Data

Hyde, Natalie, 1963-
  Cultural traditions in Sweden / Natalie Hyde.
     pages cm. -- (Cultural traditions in my world)
  Includes index.
  ISBN 978-0-7787-8064-9 (reinforced library binding) --
ISBN 978-0-7787-8069-4 (pbk.) --
ISBN 978-1-4271-9962-1 (electronic pdf) --
ISBN 978-1-4271-9957-7 (electronic html)
1. Holidays--Sweden--Juvenile works. 2. Sweden--Social life and customs--Juvenile works. I. Title.

  GT4861.A2H84 2015
  394.2609485--dc23
                                    2014045061

Crabtree Publishing Company

Printed in Canada/042015/EF20150224

www.crabtreebooks.com   1-800-387-7650

Published in Canada
Crabtree Publishing
616 Welland Ave.
St. Catharines, ON
L2M 5V6

Published in the United States
Crabtree Publishing
PMB 59051
350 Fifth Avenue, 59th Floor
New York, New York 10118

Published in the United Kingdom
Crabtree Publishing
Maritime House
Basin Road North, Hove
BN41 1WR

Published in Australia
Crabtree Publishing
3 Charles Street
Coburg North
VIC 3058

Contents

Welcome to Sweden

Sweden is a long, narrow **Scandinavian** country located between Norway and Finland in northern Europe. People have lived in Sweden for over 10,000 years. The country's official language is Swedish. There are also five **minority** languages: Finnish, Meänkieli, Sami, Yiddish, and Romani. Today, more than nine million people live in Sweden. Most people live in the southern parts of the country in or near large cities.

Colorful buildings make up the *Gamla Stan*, or Old Town, in Stockholm, the capital of Sweden.

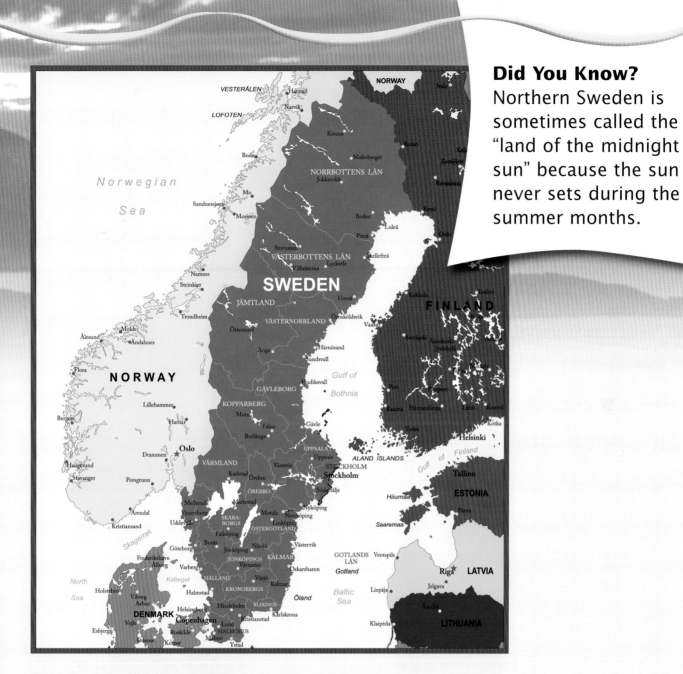

Swedes celebrate many festivals, special days, and customs. These cultural traditions are rooted in Sweden's long history. Most Swedes are part of the Lutheran Church. Lutheran is a **Christian** religion. Many of the country's holidays are based on the church calendar. Swedes also celebrate non-religious events, such as the changing of the seasons.

Special Days

Swedes celebrate many of the same special days that people in North America do. On *Alla hjärtans dag,* which is Swedish for Valentine's Day, Swedes give gifts and heart-shaped cookies to their loved ones. They also celebrate Halloween and *Första April*, or April Fools' Day. On people's birthdays, Swedes pamper each other with breakfast in bed. They sometimes serve a special birthday cake called *prinsesstårta*, or princess cake. It is made with jam and cream spread between layers of yellow cake. The cake is then topped with green **marzipan** so it looks smooth. If the cake is covered with yellow marzipan, it is called a *prinstårta*, or prince cake.

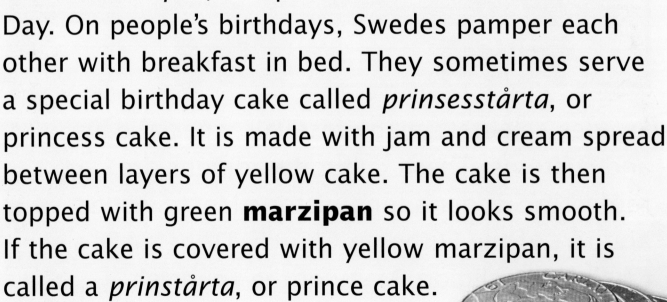

Did You Know?
On her wedding day, a Swedish bride slips silver coins in her shoes for good luck.

One of the biggest days in a student's life is their high school graduation, called *studenten.* This day is filled with excitement and singing. Students wear special caps and attend a graduation ceremony. After the ceremony, the school doors open and the students meet their families waiting outside. Parents and siblings hold up posters showing baby pictures of the graduates and hang little gifts on ribbons around the graduates' necks.

After the graduation ceremony, students spend the rest of the day riding around town in trucks or on floats, celebrating.

Happy New Year!

On New Year's Eve, many Swedes try to predict what the next year will bring. One traditional way is to look at cooled pieces of melted metal. Different shapes have different meanings. A ship means travel, a key suggests a new job, and a horse could mean a new car. A broken shape suggests bad luck. If the top of the shape is bubbly, it might mean a person will get lots of money. Another fun tradition is to throw your shoes. If a shoe lands pointed toward a door, it might mean moving away or a death will happen sometime in the new year.

Small pieces of lead or tin are melted over a flame and dropped into cold water to make shapes that predict what the New Year may bring.

Fireworks light up the sky over Stockholm at midnight.

The Swedish New Year is welcomed with ringing church bells, car horns honking, and colorful fireworks. Swedes wish one another a Happy New Year by saying "*Gott Nytt År!*" During the first few minutes of January 1, Swedish TV traditionally **broadcasts** the poem "Ring Out, Wild Bells" by Lord Alfred Tennyson read in Swedish.

Did You Know?
Swedes believe that if the sun shines on New Year's Day, it will be a good year.

Twelfth Night and St. Knut's Day

January 6 is known as Twelfth Night because it falls twelve nights after Christmas. In Sweden's past, this date marked the end of Christmas. St. Knut's Day is one week later, on January 13. This day honors the Danish prince Knut Lavard and his uncle Knut IV, who both became saints. Most people now wait until St. Knut's Day to celebrate the end of the Christmas season.

Did You Know?
On St. Knut's Day, some people dress up as a scarecrow, a hag, a goat, or "Old Knut" and prowl around town pulling practical jokes.

Knut IV became a **martyr** when he died for his Christian beliefs in the eleventh century.

On St. Knut's Day, Swedes have a party to celebrate taking down their Christmas trees and decorations. Children often invite their classmates to visit and play games. They also eat all the sugar cookies, gingerbread, and candy decorations off the tree. When the tree is bare, they throw it outdoors while singing a special song, which translates to:

Christmas has come to an end,
And the tree must go.
But next year once again
We shall see our dear old friend,
For he has promised us so.

Sami National Day

The Sami people have lived in the northern parts of Scandinavia since ancient times. They lived in tents and moved from place to place following the reindeer herds. Today they live in modern housing and only a few still raise reindeer. The Sami people have their own language, art, clothing, and traditions.

Reindeer have traditionally provided the Sami people with milk, food, clothing, and transportation.

Did You Know?
Yoik is traditional Sami singing. It is one of the oldest forms of music in Europe.

Sami culture is celebrated during the Kiruna Snow Festival each January. There is a big snow sculpture contest, and visitors can enjoy Sami food and music. At the Jokkmokk Market in February, people can buy handmade Sami items such as knives with bone handles and woven baskets. They can also watch reindeer races on the frozen lake. Sami National Day is celebrated on February 6. On that day, they fly the Sami flag and sing their national anthem in the Sami language.

Swedish Easter

While most Swedes are Christian, Easter is not seen as a religious holiday any more. On the Thursday before Easter, called Maundy Thursday, children dress up as Easter **hags**, or good witches. They put brightly colored scarves on their heads and paint their cheeks red and go door-to-door collecting candy or money. This tradition comes from the ancient Viking story of witches who flew to Mount Blakulla in Germany to dance with Satan on that day.

Some children will make special Easter cards and give them to their neighbors on Maundy Thursday.

Eggs are an important Easter symbol in Sweden. This tradition was brought from Germany in the 1800s.

On the night before Easter, called Easter Eve, family members gather together to eat a special meal with eggs, pickled herring, lamb, and salted cod. All the food is laid out in a *smörgåsbord*, which is a buffet of dishes where everyone can help themselves. This is also the day children get Easter eggs that are filled with candy or small toys.

Did You Know?
Swedes bring twigs into their house at Eastertime and decorate them with colored feathers. They are a sign of the **fertility** of spring and rebirth of the year.

Walpurgis Night

Walpurgis Night is celebrated on April 30. It began as a day to honor Saint Walburga, who performed miracles of healing. Like many other holidays, Walpurgis Night traditions are no longer centered on religious ideas. It has become a time to welcome spring. On Walpurgis Night, choirs sing songs about the new season and a bright future. This is also the first weekend livestock are let out to graze in the fields, and students switch from wearing their dark winter caps to white summer caps.

On Walpurgis Night, people gather around huge bonfires, which some believe keep evil spirits away. Others use these fires as a handy way to get rid of old odds and ends.

A political march through the streets of Stockholm on Labor Day.

The day after Walpurgis Night is May Day, also a national holiday. This day is also known as Labor Day. Most people have the day off work and spend time with their friends and family. In some major cities, different **political parties** march in parades and give speeches.

Did You Know?
April 30 is a double celebration because this is also the date of King Carl XVI Gustaf's birthday. Swedish flags fly everywhere as a sign of respect for the king.

National Day

Sweden's National Day is June 6. This holiday celebrates two important events in Swedish history. On June 6 in 1523, Gustav Vasa was elected king. He is called the father of modern Sweden because he helped Sweden separate from Norway and Denmark to become **independent**. It is also the day in 1809 that Sweden took on a constitution, or new set of rules for the country.

Swedes proudly wave blue-and-yellow flags at a National Day celebration in Stockholm.

King Carl XVI Gustaf and Queen Silvia at the Skansen in 2006.

To mark these two important events, people celebrate all over Sweden. Skansen is an open-air museum in Stockholm. On National Day, there is a flag ceremony and children in traditional costumes present the royal couple with bouquets. Many people also celebrate National Day with a picnic with family and friends.

Did You Know?
On June 6, there are special ceremonies around the country to welcome new Swedish citizens.

Midsummer

Midsummer is one of the most important holidays in Sweden. It is celebrated near the summer solstice, which is the longest day of the year. The summer solstice falls between June 19 and June 26. Midsummer celebrations mark the beginning of five weeks of summer holidays for many Swedes. The whole family gathers together to celebrate Midsummer.

In many Midsummer celebrations, traditional Swedish clothing is worn. This woman is wearing a crown of spring blossoms on her head.

The festivities begin with raising a maypole. A maypole is a tall pole that is decorated with flowers and ribbons. After the maypole is covered, games and dances take place around it. Later, everyone sits down to feast on the first potatoes and strawberries of the summer season.

Did You Know?
At Midsummer, children place bouquets of flowers under their pillows to dream about their future husband or wife.

Food Festivals

Many festivals throughout the year celebrate Swede's favorite foods. Sour Herring Day takes place on the third Thursday in August. *Surströmming*, or sour herring, is preserved by canning the fish in salt water. This dish is traditionally eaten with a thin, flat bread and boiled potatoes.

When a tin of sour herring is opened, the smell is so strong that most people have to eat it outside!

Herring is a popular dish to eat year-round in Sweden.

Crayfish are similar to lobsters, only smaller.

August is also the season to feast on crayfish. *Kräftskiva*, or the Crayfish Party, marks the end of summer. People gather to enjoy crayfish, which are cooked in water or **brine** with dill. Swedes wear bibs and funny paper hats and light paper lanterns decorated with the "man in the moon."

Did You Know?
St. Martin's Day is celebrated on November 10. On this day, Swedes enjoy a roast goose feast to honor a man who hid in a pen of geese to avoid becoming **bishop**.

All Saints' Day

In Sweden, the first Saturday after October 30 is All Saints' Day. It began as a celebration of all the Christian saints who did not have their own saint day. Today it is a quiet and serious day to remember friends and relatives who have passed away. Churches also hold special services to celebrate All Saints' Day.

Did You Know?
It is impolite to speak to anyone inside a cemetery on All Saints' Day because it is a day of quiet respect.

Popular winter sports in Sweden include skiing and ice hockey.

On All Saints' Day, many people place lighted candles or lanterns on their family graves in cemeteries. Flowers and wreaths are also used to decorate graves and headstones. As night falls, the lights form beautiful patterns in the snow. The date also marks a happier event—it is the first day of winter and the start of the **alpine** ski season. Many people head to cottages and resorts with their families to enjoy winter sports.

Lucia Day

Lucia Day, the festival of light, is a very traditional Swedish holiday. It is celebrated on December 13 and honors St. Lucy. She was a Christian martyr who was killed in 304 A.D. because of her religious beliefs. In the past, the night before Lucia Day was also thought to be the longest night of the year. St. Lucy's feast day became a time to celebrate light returning after a long dark winter.

Two children carry lit torches during a Lucia Day celebration.

St. Lucy is known as the "bringer of light." To honor her, children parade around town dressed in white gowns. In each town, one local girl is chosen as that year's "Lucia." She wears a red sash and a crown of candles. The boys are called *stjärngosse*, or "star boys." They wear pointy hats with stars. It is a tradition for children to bring gingerbread and sweet Lucia buns to family, friends, and even patients in hospitals.

Little Christmas Eve

In Sweden, the holiday season starts four weeks before Christmas on the **First of Advent**. This is when decorations appear in markets and stores. There are straw ornaments, little Swedish flags, and colorful glass balls. A goat called a *julbock*, which is usually made of straw, has become a popular symbol of Christmas in Sweden.

The day before Christmas Eve is called "Little Christmas Eve." Presents get wrapped on this day. Rhymes are added to tags on gifts to give children a hint about what is inside. This is also when families decorate their Christmas tree. Paper flags, sugar cookies, gingerbread, and items made of straw are hung.

Did You Know? Little Christmas Eve is also called Dip Day because the family eats bread dipped in the broth of the Christmas ham, which has been boiled for Christmas Day.

Christmas Eve and Christmas Day

In Sweden, Christmas Eve is when family and friends get together. The celebration starts in the afternoon with television stations airing Christmas cartoons starring Donald Duck and other characters. After that, it is time to eat! A traditional Christmas smörgåsbord, called a *julbord*, includes ham, meatballs, little sausages, pickled herring, cheese, rye bread, and rice pudding.

During Christmas dinner, an almond is often hidden in rice pudding. The person who finds it is said to be the next one to get married.

Tomtes are popular Christmas decorations in Swedish homes. Tomte traditionally wears a red cap.

After dinner *Tomte* arrives with a bag full of presents. Tomte is a traditional bearded gnome from Scandinavian **folklore**. Today, Santa Claus might deliver the gifts instead. After all the presents are opened, families play games, sing carols, and spend time together. On Christmas Day, many people go to church, then spend the rest of the day visiting with friends and family.

Glossary

alpine Of or on the mountains

bishop A high-ranking member in the Christian church

brine Heavily salted water

broadcasts Sends out by radio or television

charities Organizations set up to help, or raise money, for those in need

Christian Someone who follows the teachings of Jesus Christ, whom they believe to be the Son of God

fertility The ability to produce new plants or animals

First of Advent The first of the four Sundays before Christmas Day

folklore Beliefs and customs from a specific group of people

independent Describing a country that makes it own laws and governs itself

martyr A person who is killed because of their religious beliefs

marzipan A sweet paste made of ground almonds and sugar

minority Being or relating to the smaller in number of two parts

political parties Groups of people who share the same ideas about how a country should be run

Scandinavian Describing the region in northern Europe that includes Norway, Sweden, Finland, Denmark, and Iceland

Index